Text copyright © 2022 by Ashley Rae Klinger. All rights reserved. Illustrated by QBN Studios. No part of this publication, including its concept and characters, may be reproduced, distributed, or transmitted in any form or by any means, including photocopying, recording, other electronic or mechanical methods, or by information storage and retrieval system, without prior written permission of the author and publisher, except in the case of brief quotations embodied in reviews and certain other non-commercial uses permitted by copyright law. The concept of the Family Shrub and the "shrub not a tree" philosophy was uniquely created and is the intellectual property of Ashley Rae Klinger and It's Her Brand Enterprises.

Message Mission

With the ability to develop meaningful messages and life-changing platforms, while appropriately and effectively sharing and promoting those messages and platforms with audiences around the world, author Ashley Rae (Klinger) has introduced **A Shrub Not a Tree** as the first book in a special collection of children's books inspired by the growth of her family and their journey through *infertility*, *adoption*, and *foster care*.

Each book's message is divided into **two parts**. The first part is aimed at providing children of all ages with a thought-provoking, age-appropriate message that's easy to comprehend, while the second part is aimed at providing adults with additional insight and a deeper understanding of the overall concept and mindset behind that message; in the hopes of empowering and equipping all families with the desire and ability to not only initiate conversations with one another about that particular message, as it pertains to their family or a family they may know, but to live **purposeful**, **intentional**, **engaged**, and **faith-filled** lives – as individuals and as families.

"Ashley Rae is an inspiring person and now author. She is someone that takes on life's challenges and finds ways in which to make this world a better place. Her kind and generous heart is an inspiration to many. She has found ways in which to use her compassion for others, her knowledge of marketing and message delivery, and her public speaking ability to impact individuals, families, companies and communities in a positive way. While some may roll over and give up when presented the obstacles placed in front of Ashley and her husband, she has chosen to rise up, listen to God's plan for her and her family's life, and make the best of situations. Her positive attitude and unwavering faith in God is demonstrated not only in her writing, but in her daily life as well. This world is a better place because of Ashley Rae and I love seeing her charge to inspire others to make it better as well." ~ Carma Hanson | Safe Kids Coordinator and Child Safety Advocate.

Dedicated to Our Four Little Leaves

This book is dedicated to the four beautiful leaves who made our Family Shrub possible by helping us become the parents and the family we've grown to be. Micah, Kinzie, Luna, and Serenity; even on the most challenging of days, the four of you make our lives better in every way. We are beyond grateful God entrusted us with the privilege and the responsibility of being your parents. Our shrub wouldn't be fully grown without each of your leaves. Remember to always trust and lean fully on the Lord for guidance, support, and nourishment in every circumstance throughout life.

We'll love you always ~ Mommy Ashley & Daddy Andrew

A Special Thank You

A special thank you to all of those who have helped our Family Shrub grow. To the other foster families of our children who cared for them before they came into our care. To the many professionals who trusted our abilities to love and serve our children and who passionately advocated for them and our family. To our community of fellow foster and adoptive families who share in our experiences. To the birth families of our children who selflessly want the best life possible for each of them. To our family and friends who continue to support us throughout our journey. Above all to God for His ever-constant love and grace; for allowing us the opportunity to love and serve as parents and as a family by grooming, pruning, and shaping us into the family we have grown to be; for the endless blessings and opportunities that He provides to our family that allow us to grow together, to lead by example, to make a difference in the lives of others, and to love and serve His people as HE sees fit.

Introduction

Inspired by the growth of her family and their journey through *infertility*, *adoption*, and *foster care*, author Ashley Rae (Klinger) has introduced **A Shrub Not a Tree** as the first book in a special collection of children's books aimed at empowering and equipping families around the world to live **purposeful, intentional, engaged,** and **faith-filled** lives.

What started as a "legacy project" for her family transformed into a relatable message that families around the world can embrace and apply to the growth of their own families. The initial concept and inspiration for **A Shrub Not a Tree** grew through her (and her husband's) desire to understand, as parents, how to initiate conversations with their four adopted children that would help them understand their family's story and the circumstances that contribute to their family's dynamic. They also wanted to help their young children recognize that although their family may grow differently than some, their family, like **every** family, is planted with a purpose and is equally important to God and His kingdom.

Through the simple comparison of a shrub and a tree, Ashley Rae developed the "nontraditional" **Family Shrub** as an alternative concept to the "traditional" **Family Tree** to celebrate the different ways that families grow to be. The concept of the **Family Shrub** and the **"shrub not a tree"** philosophy is not meant to chop down the **Family Tree**. Instead, it's meant to provide **all** families with a way to embrace the *growth* and *intentional blessing* of **their** family, and to help them recognize that their *inability* to add a leaf in what some consider the "traditional way" to a TREE, doesn't define them as a FAMILY. Rather, it's their *ability* to achieve God's **purpose** for planting **their** family.

Whether they've grown to be a shrub or a tree, Ashley Rae guides families through a creative **two-step process** that demonstrates how families can work together *as a team* to **grow together** in their relationships with one another and to **reach their maturity and full blooming potential** as individuals and as families, to achieve God's **purpose** for planting their family. In step one, she helps readers understand the importance of recognizing how to **LOVE** *abundantly* in order to **grow together** in their relationships with one another - and with God. To do so, she demonstrates how to replace *weeds of negativity* with positivity by **identifying their weeds, picking their weeds**, and **nurturing their gardens** in order to *multiply* goodness in their relationships. In step two, she helps readers understand the importance of recognizing how to **SERVE** *selflessly* and *intentionally* in order to **reach their maturity and full blooming potential** as individuals and as families. To do so, she demonstrates how to recognize and **pair together** their God-granted *abilities* and *opportunities* in the most appropriate and effective ways in order to be *fruitful* in their efforts to glorify God.

A Shrub Not a Tree features a **two-part approach** to provide children of all ages with a thought-provoking, age-appropriate message that's easy to comprehend, while also providing adults with additional insight and a deeper understanding of the message and overall mindset behind the concept of the **Family Shrub** and the **"shrub not a tree"** philosophy.

"Whether our families grow to be more of a shrub or more of a tree, we are all a part of God's kingdom and His one big family!" ~ Ashley Rae (Klinger)

I'm Mommy Ashley, and I'm Daddy Andrew. This is a special story about **our** FAMILY and how God groomed, pruned, and shaped us into the Family SHRUB, not the Family TREE, that **our** FAMILY has grown to be.

Like **every** SHRUB and TREE, the growth of **every** FAMILY is different and unique, but **every** FAMILY growing near and far is equally important in the role they play in God's one big FAMILY. Like **every** SHRUB and TREE, God plants **every** FAMILY with a **purpose** to achieve. And, through His LOVE and GRACE, He provides **every** FAMILY with the nourishment, tools, and techniques they need to succeed.

By sharing the story of how **our** FAMILY has grown to be, we hope to help other FAMILIES see how they too can achieve God's **purpose** for planting their FAMILY...

...whether it be as a
FAMILY SHRUB or as a FAMILY TREE.

Long before we became parents, we knew that we wanted to have a FAMILY. Like many moms and dads do, we imagined what it would be like to watch **our** FAMILY TREE grow.

We imagined feeling excited when we found out that we were adding a new leaf to **our** FAMILY TREE by having a baby. We imagined sharing and celebrating the exciting news of our baby with FAMILY and friends.

We imagined bringing our baby home from the hospital. We imagined cuddling and rocking our baby in their new room.

We even imagined watching our baby grow; admiring the unique similarities between us, and the special **connection** that we would share as members of the same FAMILY.

Although we were excited for **our FAMILY TREE** to grow, it didn't happen how we imagined it would. In fact, after we learned that we couldn't have babies like we wanted to, there was a sad time when we didn't know if **our FAMILY TREE** would grow at all.

Day and night, we prayed as we watched **other** FAMILY TREES grow all around us. Although we didn't understand why **our** FAMILY TREE wouldn't grow how **we** imagined it to be, we continued to trust God's faithful plan - and the power of His mighty hand. During prayer, God gently reminded us that, just like SHRUBS and TREES, some FAMILIES grow in different ways – but their **purpose** for being planted remains the **same**.

With a whole lot of patience and a lot more prayer, our FAMILY started to grow, and it grew in the most unexpected way. Through the blessings of His LOVE and GRACE, God groomed, pruned, and shaped our FAMILY into this SHRUB rather than this TREE, as we first imagined it would grow to be.

As our SHRUB grew over time, God planted in our hearts the "**shrub not a tree**" philosophy to help **our** FAMILY and others see the *growth* and *blessing of* **our** FAMILY. By sharing this philosophy with FAMILIES growing near and far, our hope is **not** for the FAMILY SHRUB to chop down the FAMILY TREE. Instead, our hope is for **other** FAMILIES to see the *growth* and *blessing* of **every** FAMILY, while helping them to achieve God's **purpose** for planting **their** FAMILY; whether it grows to be more of a SHRUB or more of a TREE.

To help us understand how different FAMILIES grow to be, let's take a closer look at the **"shrub not a tree"** philosophy.

Just as we first expected **our** FAMILY would grow to be, many FAMILIES around the world grow similar to this TREE, which represents the growth and history of a **whole** FAMILY.

From the **roots**, to the *trunk*, to the **branches**, to the **leaves**, each part of a FAMILY TREE represents a part of that **same** FAMILY. At the center of the FAMILY TREE is the **one** FAMILY TRUNK, which represents the structure and design of that **one** FAMILY; linking its members living years ago to its members today as they continue to grow. From grandparents, parents, brothers, sisters, aunts, uncles, cousins, and their children too, the members of a FAMILY TREE are **connected** through **their** FAMILY DNA. Unique to just **their** FAMILY, their DNA flows through **their** TREE from the **roots**, to the *trunk*, to the **branches**, to the **leaves**; connecting **their entire** FAMILY.

Different than how **we** expected it would grow to be, **our** FAMILY grew similar to this SHRUB rather than that TREE. Although a FAMILY SHRUB represents the growth and history of a **whole** FAMILY, it does so a little differently than a FAMILY TREE.

From the **roots**, to the *stems*, to the **branches**, to the **leaves**, each part of a FAMILY SHRUB represents a part of **different** FAMILIES. At the center of the FAMILY SHRUB is **more than one** FAMILY STEM, which represents the structure and design of **more than one** FAMILY. From biological, adoptive, foster, step, and blended too, those **different** FAMILY **stems** overlap and intertwine; linking members of **more than one** FAMILY living years ago to members of **more than one** FAMILY today as they continue to grow. From grandparents, parents, brothers, sisters, aunts, uncles, cousins, and their children too, the members of a FAMILY SHRUB may **not** be connected by their FAMILY DNA like the members of a FAMILY TREE. Instead, the members of a FAMILY SHRUB are **connected** by **their** FAMILY **LOVE**. Unique to just **their** FAMILY, their **LOVE** flows through **their** SHRUB from the **roots**, to the *stems*, to the **branches**, to the **leaves**; connecting **their entire** FAMILY.

One **root**, **stem**, **branch**, and **leaf** at a time, the structure of **our** FAMILY grew into a SHRUB with an intricate design. While some parts sprouted a little different than some, we've come to realize that **every** part of **our** SHRUB has a role to play that is essential to the *growth* and **purpose** of **our** one big FAMILY.

God's **purpose** for planting **our** FAMILY is the *same* as all the rest; to **grow together** and to **reach OUR maturity** and full blooming potential as an **entire** FAMILY; whether it be as a SHRUB or as a TREE. Although that **purpose** may seem complicated to some, God's **purpose** for every FAMILY can be easily achieved when we rely on His nourishment and the use of certain tools and techniques.

To help us better understand a **FAMILY'S purpose** and how to succeed, let's take a closer look at two simple steps and a few of those different tools and techniques.

The first step to achieve our **purpose** as a **FAMILY** is to **grow together** in our **RELATIONSHIPS** with one another *as a team*.

To do so, we must *multiply* and *scatter* our seeds of LOVE *abundantly*. But first, we must recognize that the different ways in which weeds hurt the growth of our SHRUBS and TREES is similar to the ways in which *negativity* hurts the growth of our RELATIONSHIPS and our FAMILIES. Although this will look different for **every FAMILY**, we can all learn how to **identify** and **pick the weeds** of *negativity* so that LOVE spreads more freely. Once the *weeds of negativity* are spotted and removed, we must then **nurture our gardens** *tenderly* with lots of *positivity* to prevent the weeds from growing back in our RELATIONSHIPS and our FAMILIES.

Can you **identify** some *weeds of negativity*? How can you **pick** them? How can you **nurture your gardens**?

The second step to achieve our purpose as a FAMILY is to reach OUR maturity and full blooming potential with one another *as a team*.

To do so, we must be *fruitful* through the ways that we SERVE *selflessly* and *intentionally*. But first, we must recognize that the different ways in which SHRUBS and TREES serve the world is similar to the ways in which we all SERVE the world as INDIVIDUALS and as FAMILIES. Although this will look different for **every FAMILY**, we can all learn how to **pair together** our own unique *abilities* and *opportunities* to SERVE God - in different ways, at different times, and for different reasons why.

What are some unique *abilities* and *opportunities* and how can they be paired **together** to make a difference in the world?

Although it was difficult for us to originally see, our *inability* to add a leaf to a TREE doesn't define us as a FAMILY. Instead, our FAMILY is defined by our *ability* to work together *as a team* to achieve God's **purpose** for planting **our** FAMILY.

Through the example of how **our** FAMILY has grown to be and the ways in which we've worked together *as a team*, we hope to help **other** FAMILIES see how they too can work together *as a team* to define **their** FAMILY; whether it be as a SHRUB or as a TREE.

Whether our FAMILIES grow to be more of a SHRUB or more of a TREE, we are ALL a part of God's kingdom and His one big FAMILY!

To Our Adult Readers...This is Our Journey

As a couple who has been impacted by infertility, I struggled with our story for a while; probably more so than Andrew struggled. As a woman, not being able to conceive children left me feeling like a failure in so many ways. There was a point in our journey when I felt lost; I felt defective; I felt broken; I felt inadequate; I felt "less than" capable and worthy as other women; I felt like I was letting my husband and my family down; I felt as though I was maybe being "punished" for all the "wrongs" I did in my life. Despite those and many other feelings, I, and we, remained faithful. As a couple of faith who trust in the bigger plan that we cannot always see and do not always understand, we stayed committed to putting our trust in God's plan for our lives and for our family. Together and alone, Andrew and I spent countless hours in prayer asking God to help us conceive a child. Then one day God placed a question on my heart during prayer that changed the course of our lives forever; "Do you want to be pregnant, or do you want to be parents?" The answer was simple; we wanted to be parents.

In that moment of prayer, God was able to provide us with clarity. He transformed our hearts and our minds to help us see that our family and our role as parents isn't defined by our *inability* to conceive, but rather by our *ability* to simply **love** and **serve** others. In that moment, God reminded us that we've all been called to **love** and **serve** His people, rather than to be served by them, and we're meant to **love** and **serve** in whatever unique ways HE sees fit. It was then when our prayers changed from; "please help us to conceive a child" to "please help us to love and serve as parents as You see fit."

After a seven-year on-going journey through infertility, adoption, and foster care, we are now blessed to be the parents of four adopted children; Micah (6), who was placed in our home through foster care in 2017 and we adopted in 2018, and a sibling group of three girls; Kinzie (5), Luna (4), and Serenity (4), who were placed in our home through foster care in 2019 and we adopted in 2021. It was our journey through infertility that led us to our journey through adoption, which led us to our journey through foster care - and then again through adoption.

Infertility didn't prevent us from becoming parents; it just changed HOW we became them and WHO we became them to. Our inability to conceive and give birth to our children doesn't define us as their parents, nor does it define us as a family. We might not be a family by blood, but we are a family through LOVE. Ultimately, our *inability* to conceive was a BLESSING as it gave us the *ability* to **embrace** our story and to **leverage** it in ways that allow us to grow together. We have also been afforded the opportunity to lead by example, to make a positive difference in our lives and in the lives of others, and to love and serve God's people as a FAMILY, all while **trusting** and **leaning** fully on the Lord throughout our journey.

As a woman, will I always wonder what it feels like to carry and give birth to a child, and are there aspects about fatherhood that Andrew may always be curious about? Naturally; but "missing out" on those experiences no longer bothers us as it did in the past because God helped us realize that the few experiences that we **won't** have has opened the door to the many experiences and *countless blessings* that we **will** have.

One of those experiences and blessings is sharing our story. As a couple, we continue to openly share our family's story and our journey with infertility, adoption, and foster care. We don't do it because we're looking for validation, praise, or recognition, nor do we do it because we feel that our family is any better or any more deserving of God's love and grace than the next family. We do it to simply **fulfill** what we believe to be God's *will* for our lives and to **inspire** others to stay rooted in their faith, to trust God's bigger plan, and to lean fully on the Lord in all circumstances; even when all hope seems lost. We do it to **provide** hope to those like us who have been impacted by infertility, yet long to be the parents and the family they were meant to be, and to **remind** them that their inability to give birth to children doesn't define them as parents or as a family. Rather, they're defined by the LOVE they share and by their ability and willingness to answer God's call to SERVE one another. And, finally, we do it to **be a voice** for all the children and families in the world who we're all called to LOVE and SERVE through foster care and/or through adoption.

Our journey has been, and continues to be, both incredibly rewarding and incredibly challenging for a variety of reasons. Although challenging, we wouldn't change a thing about it because we know God's faithful plan is always better than our own, and we remind ourselves daily that "God doesn't call the prepared, He prepares the called." So, we continue to trust the plan that we cannot always see and do not always understand, and we continue to ask God to **guide us** where HE wants us to go, to **provide us** with what we need along the way, and to **protect us** on the journey. We continue to embrace OUR story and OUR journey because without it we wouldn't have the opportunity to LOVE and SERVE the children and the families that we do, and we wouldn't have become the FAMILY **we** have grown to be.

Our FAMILY may be more of a SHRUB than a TREE, but this is the FAMILY **we** have grown to be; a FAMILY groomed, pruned, and shaped by God's love and grace and defined by the LOVE we share and the ways in which we're called to SERVE one another.

This is Our Hope

As a family who has been shaped by a journey through infertility, adoption, and foster care, we found it difficult to find just one resource that fully encompassed the message that we wanted to share with our children. With that goal in mind, the initial concept and inspiration for this book was born, and then grew through our desire to simply understand, as parents, how to initiate conversations with our children about our family's story, while helping them to make sense of the circumstances that contribute to the dynamics of our family. More importantly, we wanted to help our children recognize that, although different from some families, OUR family, like any family, is an *intentional blessing* from God, and OUR family is equally as special and important to God and His kingdom as the next family. To help us fill those needs for our own family, God sowed in our hearts the concept of the **Family Shrub** and the **"shrub not a tree"** philosophy to help us not only embrace the *growth* and *intentional blessing* of OUR family, but to also help us achieve His **purpose** for planting OUR family. In doing so, it ultimately helped us make deeper **connections** with one another as a family and provided us with a sense of **identity**, **belonging**, and **understanding**.

Our hope for sharing our concept of the **Family Shrub** and the **"shrub not a tree"** philosophy, while being open and honest about our own imperfect and ever-evolving journey, is multidimensional.

* **As the "nontraditional" family that we've grown to be, our hope** is to use our story to now **inspire** and **encourage** all families, especially families like ours, to embrace the *growth* and *intentional blessing* of THEIR family, while also helping them to achieve God's **purpose** for planting THEIR family; whether it be as a SHRUB or as a TREE. By doing so, we hope to help them make deeper **connections** with one another as a family, while providing them with that sense of **identity**, **belonging**, and **understanding** for which they too may be searching.

* **As parents to our four adopted children who came to us through foster care**, we were not provided with a "rule book" as to how to navigate this journey, which has taught us that every circumstance, every family, and every relationship will be different and will change over time. As their parents, we're simply doing our best to navigate this journey in a way that we believe is healthy and appropriate for everyone involved; especially, **our** family. By sharing a glimpse into our approach to navigating the *seasons* of this ever-evolving journey, **our hope** is to **inspire** and **encourage** other parents to initiate open, honest, age-appropriate, faith-filled conversations with their children about their life and their circumstances; whatever those circumstances may be. By being open and honest with children from an early point in their journey, we can help alleviate confusion and self-doubt in the future; we can help empower them to **embrace** their story and to **leverage** their circumstances and their God-granted *abilities* and *opportunities* in ways that will allow THEM to make a positive difference in their life and in the lives of others; we can be an example for them and teach them how to **trust** and **lean** fully on the Lord in every circumstance throughout life, and to **recognize** THEIR true identity in Him and in Him alone.

* **As parents who did not contribute to the biological birth of our four adopted children**, we encounter situations, challenges, and emotions every day that many other parents do not; including when and how to foster relationships with members of our children's different families. By sharing a glimpse into our approach to fostering multi-dimensional relationships with other family members, **our hope** is to **inspire** and **encourage** other parents to open their minds and their hearts to the possibility of ever-evolving relationships between them, their children, and members of their different families; as long as those relationships are, and remain, healthy, appropriate, safe, and beneficial to both the short-term and long-term growth and development of their children. Although we have every right to be protective of our children, our own fears and insecurities about other family members can, at times, get in the way of doing what may be best for them. We know this because we have also had those feelings at some point in our journey. By being real and transparent about those feelings, **our hope** is to also **inspire** and **encourage** others with similar circumstances to turn any of their own "unproductive" feelings over to the Lord and to remember that all children, including our own, are God's children. He entrusted us with the privilege and the responsibility to love and serve them by nurturing them, protecting them, guiding them, and helping them become the people God created THEM to be, which may require US to work through our own feelings in order to foster relationships with members of their different families - if and when appropriate.

* **As hopeful parents who had their own "ideas" and "plans" as to how our family was going to grow to be**, we were initially discouraged when those ideas and plans didn't come to fruition as WE thought they should. However, through our journey, we were reminded to "let go and let God" and to loosen the "grip of control" that we had on our lives in order to fully surrender to Him in EVERY circumstance. By sharing a glimpse into our approach to surrendering our lives to the Lord on a daily basis, **our final hope** is to **inspire** and **encourage** other hopeful parents to do the same and to consider growing their own **Family Shrub**. This can be done by opening their minds, their hearts, and their homes to children in foster care and/or those in need of a stable and nurturing family unit through adoption.

This is Our "Shrub not a Tree" Philosophy

The Concept and Design of a Family Tree

By various definitions, genealogy is defined as a line of descent traced continuously from one ancestor to the next, and an ancestor is defined as any person from whom one has descended *biologically*. To track and chart a person's line of decent, we often use a genealogical tree; better known as a **Family Tree**. By various definitions, a **Family Tree** is a diagram showing the biological connection and relationship between people in several generations of a family. Simply put, a **Family Tree** represents the growth and history of a **whole** family.

In other words, we often think of a **Family Tree** in reference to members of the **same** family who are **connected** and related to one another by their DNA - their blood, passed down from one biological family member to the next over generations. Their DNA **connects** them as a family to their past, their present, and their future. The concept of a **Family Tree** can often provide the members of a family with a deeper **connection** to one another, with a sense of **identity** and **belonging**, and with an **understanding** of where, and from whom, one comes. For individuals who have contributed to the biological birth of a child, it can also provide them with a sense of **purpose**; knowing they have added a leaf to their branch on their **Family's Tree**, which extends the growth and history of **their** family.

For nonbiological parents like us and "nontraditional" families like ours, the concept of a **Family Tree** can be difficult to embrace. For instance, if the six members of our "immediate" family researched each of our individual, genealogical **Family Trees**, we would not all be "**connected**" to one another. Andrew and Micah would be connected, as the two of them share DNA as second cousins, and Kinzie, Luna, and Serenity would be connected, as the three of them share DNA as full, biological sisters - as they were born with the same biological mother and the same biological father. However, Micah and the girls would not be connected to one another, nor would Andrew and the girls be connected to one another. And, as for me, I wouldn't be connected to any of them, as I don't share a single strand of DNA with any members of our immediate family. That feeling of **DISconnection** can make us question our **identity** and where we **belong** in **our** family. It can also create feelings of confusion as we try to **understand** the dynamics of our particular family and our **purpose** in it, all of which can initiate many "negative" or "unproductive" emotions for everyone involved and for different reasons.

For example, **as children ourselves**, we may experience feelings of guilt because we're not biologically contributing to the next generation of our ancestor's Family Tree; ending the growth and future of our family. **As nonbiological parents of children**, we may experience feelings of sadness or inadequacy because we're not "connected" to our children in the same way that their other family members are connected to them. We may experience feelings of worry that, as our children grow older, they may question their identity, their circumstances, and their place in our family. We may also experience feelings of rejection or insecurities if our children ever discard the role we've taken on as their parents, and the ways in which we've contributed to their lives; the list of emotions is endless and can be overwhelming at times.

Just as **we** are prone to experience a multitude of feelings, **our children** may experience them too. These may include feelings such as confusion, abandonment, anger, resentment, and self-doubt, among others. And, let's not forget about **members of our children's different families**. They may also experience feelings such as guilt, worry, and sadness, just to name a few.

Although we have shared a handful of "negative" emotions potentially experienced by "nontraditional" families navigating infertility, adoption, and foster care, there are admittedly many, if not more, positive emotions that our family has experienced. However, we're highlighting the "negative" in relation to the journey of our nontraditional family and **our** immediate family's "non-existing" **Family Tree** because it's the "negative" that ultimately stunts the growth and development of our families in many different ways. Throughout our journey, we've been reminded that with every "negative" emotion and circumstance, there can be an opportunity for growth and a positive outcome. Our family's journey continues to be a testament to both of those truths.

Recognizing and processing emotions related to the journey of any family and their circumstances is an important part of their overall growth and development and their ability to not only cope through their family's circumstances, but to embrace whatever outcomes follow. For that reason, we don't want to necessarily change or eliminate any emotions or circumstances in another family's journey. Instead, we want to simply support and nurture their journey by giving them an alternative concept to the traditional **Family Tree**, one that will hopefully help them embrace the *growth* and *intentional blessing* of THEIR family - regardless of how it's grown to be.

A Shrub versus a Tree

Although similar in some ways, shrubs and trees are quite different, yet, equally important and meaningful to the world around them. They both have been *intentionally* planted by God, they both grow as an intricate part of His kingdom. They each serve unique purposes to the environment such as shade, shelter, color, fragrance, protection, and overall beauty to the landscape. Although the structure and growth cycles of a shrub and a tree are different, they can both grow together and reach their maturity and full blooming potential when nourished by their Creator.

Most trees are tall, their **roots** connect to ONE **trunk**, and their distinct **branches**, although surrounded by **leaves,** are usually visible and easy to see. As new branches sprout over time, their origin can still be easily tracked back to the tree's ONE trunk. As a tree continues to grow, its structure remains dependent on its trunk, and although it can be somewhat groomed and pruned, its overall shape and design doesn't really change over time. Although there are a wide variety of trees that are unique in their own way, most trees are generally slower growing and often require a longer period of time to reach their maturity and full blooming potential.

Whereas most shrubs are shorter, their **roots** connect to MANY **stems**, and their many **branches**, hidden behind its **leaves**, are usually difficult to see as they overlap and intertwine to create the shrub's unique structure and intricate design. As new stems and branches sprout over time, they add to the multidimensional intricacy of the shrub. As a result, the origin of each branch becomes more difficult to track back to one of the stems. As the shrub continues to grow, its structure remains dependent on **not one trunk**, but on its MANY main stems - and with the ability to be groomed and pruned, its overall shape and design can change over time. Although there are a wide variety of shrubs that are unique in their own way, most are generally faster growing and require a shorter time to reach their maturity and full blooming potential.

A Family Shrub versus a Family Tree

Through the simple comparison of a SHRUB and a TREE, the concept of the FAMILY SHRUB and the **"shrub not a tree"** philosophy started to grow. Although similar in many ways, a FAMILY SHRUB and a FAMILY TREE are also quite different and yet equally important and meaningful to the world around them.

As previously mentioned, a FAMILY TREE represents the growth and history of a **whole** family. From the **roots**, **trunk**, **branches**, and **leaves**, each part of a FAMILY TREE represents a part of that **same** FAMILY. At the center of the FAMILY TREE is the **one** FAMILY **TRUNK**, which represents the structure and design of that **one** FAMILY; linking its members living years ago to its members today as they continue to grow. From grandparents, parents, brothers, sisters, aunts, uncles, cousins, and their children too, the members of a FAMILY TREE are **connected** through **their** FAMILY **DNA**. Unique to just **their** FAMILY, their **DNA** flows through **their** TREE from the **roots**, to the **trunk**, to the **branches**, to the **leaves**, connecting their **entire** FAMILY.

Although a FAMILY SHRUB also represents the growth and history of a **whole** FAMILY, it does so a little differently than a FAMILY TREE. From the **roots**, **stems**, **branches**, and **leaves**, each part of a FAMILY SHRUB represents a part of **different** FAMILIES. At the center of the FAMILY SHRUB is **more than one** FAMILY **STEM**, which represents the structure and design of **more than one** different FAMILY. From biological, adoptive, foster, step, and blended too, those different FAMILY **stems** overlap and intertwine; linking members of **more than one** FAMILY living years ago to members of **more than one** FAMILY today as they continue to grow. From grandparents, parents, brothers, sisters, aunts, uncles, cousins, and their children too, the members of a FAMILY SHRUB may **not** be connected by their FAMILY **DNA**, as that is something that they may **not** all share as with the members of a FAMILY TREE. Rather, the members of a FAMILY SHRUB are **connected** by **their** FAMILY **LOVE**. Unique to just **their** FAMILY, their **LOVE** flows through **their** SHRUB from the **roots**, to the **stems**, to the **branches**, to the **leaves**, connecting their **entire** FAMILY.

Planted with a Purpose

One **root**, **stem**, **branch**, and **leaf** at a time, the structure of **our own** FAMILY grew into a SHRUB with an intricate design. Through the growth of **our** FAMILY, God taught us this; while some parts *sprouted* a little differently than others, **every** part of **our** SHRUB has a role to play that is essential to the *growth* and **purpose** of our one big FAMILY. Whether a FAMILY has grown to be a SHRUB or a TREE, that same rule applies; **every** member of a FAMILY has a role to play that is essential to the *growth* and **purpose** of THEIR one big FAMILY.

According to the Book of Genesis, God's **purpose** for planting a FAMILY is the same as all the rest; **to be fruitful and to multiply**. In other words, we're intended to have children as they continue the *life* of our FAMILIES and the existence of mankind. For those who cannot conceive and/or give birth to biological children, the concept of being *fruitful* and *multiplying* can be difficult to embrace. However, throughout our journey, God has helped us to see that the ways in which families are *fruitful*, and the ways in which they *multiply*, isn't limited to conception and birth alone. **Every** FAMILY has the ability to be *fruitful* and to *multiply* according to *how* and *what* they contribute to God's kingdom.

Ultimately, God's **purpose** for planting FAMILIES, as **we've** grown to see it, is to **grow together** and to **reach OUR maturity and full blooming potential** as an **entire** FAMILY; whether it be as a SHRUB or as a TREE.

Although that **purpose** may seem complicated to some, when we learn to rely on God's LOVE and GRACE to help groom, prune, and shape us into the FAMILIES we're meant to be, His **purpose** for planting our FAMILIES can be easily achieved. To help us better understand **every** FAMILY'S **purpose** and how to succeed, let's take a closer look at two simple steps and a few different tools and techniques.

Step One in achieving our **purpose** as a FAMILY is to work together *as a team* to **grow together** in our RELATIONSHIPS with one another – and with God. To do so, we must *answer the call* to *multiply* positivity and all things good in our RELATIONSHIPS by *scattering* our seeds of **LOVE** *abundantly*. For a variety of reasons, that isn't always easy to do as our relationships are often complicated and difficult to navigate. However, through the example of God's one and only son, we are reminded to "love because He first loved us" and are provided with examples of how to do so. Although this will look different for **every** FAMILY, we can all *multiply* positivity and goodness by sharing our LOVE more *abundantly*, tending to our relationships, and **growing together** in them.

* To begin, we must first **identify the weeds** of *negativity* that are growing in our relationships. The ways in which weeds can *hurt* our SHRUBS and TREES is similar to the ways in which *weeds of negativity* can *hurt* our RELATIONSHIPS and the members of our FAMILIES. Therefore, it's important for us to **identify** what those *weeds of negativity* are, and *where* and *why* they're growing. **Identifying the weeds** will look different for **every** FAMILY. Not only can weeds take on many forms, but they can grow in different places and for various reasons. Some can even disguise themselves, making it difficult to **identify** them. A few examples of negative weeds are outside influences, the actions and attitudes of others, our behaviors and choices, and even emotions such as anger, sadness, guilt, resentment, insecurity, comparison, and jealousy.

* Once the *weeds of negativity* are identified, we must then **pick the weeds** to remove the *negativity* from our RELATIONSHIPS – and from our daily lives. The ways in which weeds can *stunt* the growth and development of SHRUBS and TREES is similar to the ways in which *weeds of negativity* can *stunt* the growth and development of our RELATIONSHIPS with one another. Therefore, it's important for us to **pick** those weeds by understanding the most effective and appropriate methods to do so. **Picking the weeds** will look different for **every** FAMILY. Not only will different weeds require various tools and techniques to **pick** them, but some will be more challenging than others and may have the ability to grow back despite being removed. A few examples of those tools and techniques are eliminating distractions, acknowledging the ways we've been offended, being honest about our own offenses, and even consulting a spiritual advisor, counselor, or coach.

* Once the *weeds of negativity* are picked, we must remember to **nurture our gardens** with lots of *positivity* and goodness. Our "gardens" in this case are referring to our FAMILIES and our RELATIONSHIPS with one another. The many benefits of **nurturing** our SHRUBS

and TREES are similar to those of tending to our FAMILIES and our RELATIONSHIPS, **nurturing** them according to their specific needs. **Nurturing our gardens** will look different for **every** FAMILY. Depending on the nature of our weeds, there are various tools and techniques that we can use to **nurture our gardens**, preventing our weeds from growing back and allowing our FAMILIES and RELATIONSHIPS the opportunity to not just survive – but *thrive*. A few examples of those tools and techniques are setting boundaries, surrounding ourselves with individuals and FAMILIES who provide a positive growing environment, maintaining a suitable work-life balance, re-evaluating priorities, or joining a Bible study or other positive activities. Additional examples include providing emotional support to others and fostering positive emotions such as forgiveness, gratitude, respect, compassion, patience, and understanding.

Step Two in achieving our **purpose** as a FAMILY is to work together *as a team* to **reach OUR maturity and full blooming potential** - as individuals and as families. To do so, we must *answer the call* to be *fruitful* in our efforts and in the ways in which we **SERVE** *selflessly* and *intentionally*. For a variety of reasons, that isn't always easy to do, as our lives are often complicated and difficult to navigate. However, through the example of God's one and only son, we are reminded to live a life that glorifies God and are provided with examples of how to do so. Although this will look different for **every** FAMILY, we can all be *fruitful* in our efforts to **SERVE** when we learn how to **pair together** our God-granted *abilities* and *opportunities* in ways that glorify God. This will help us to **reach OUR maturity and full blooming potential**.

Throughout life, God will call upon all of us to **SERVE** in *different ways*, at *different times*, and for *different reasons why*.
* To help us answer those calls, God will grant us with unique *abilities*, both as individuals and as FAMILIES. Those *abilities* are a combination of our own gifts, talents, passions, experiences, and resources. Whatever those *abilities* may be, they're meant to be utilized and not wasted.
* To help us utilize those *abilities*, God will grant us with appropriate *opportunities* that are unique to OUR *abilities*. Those *opportunities* will allow us to be *fruitful* in our efforts and in the ways in which we choose to **SERVE**. Whatever those *opportunities* may be, they're meant to be pursued and not ignored.

The ways in which SHRUBS and TREES are *fruitful* and **SERVE** the world are similar to the ways in which we can all be *fruitful* and **SERVE** the world - as individuals and as FAMILIES. However, not all of our *abilities* and *opportunities* will be as obvious or as easy to **pair together** as others. Therefore, it's our responsibility, as individuals and as FAMILIES, to pray and discern which *abilities* and *opportunities* are the most appropriate and effective for **us** to **pair together** in order to produce the best fruit. There are endless ways in which we can be *fruitful* in our efforts and in the ways in which we **SERVE** *selflessly* and *intentionally*. A few examples are living by the fruits of the spirit, training up our children in His ways, giving our time, sharing our gifts and talents, lending a listening ear, supporting the less fortunate, making a financial donation, or praying for the needs of others.

When we work together *as a team* to **grow together** and to **reach OUR maturity and full blooming potential** – as individuals and as FAMILIES – we'll be better equipped to achieve God's **purpose** for planting our FAMILIES.

In closing, **our** FAMILY may be more of a SHRUB than a TREE, but this is the FAMILY **we** have grown to be; a FAMILY groomed, pruned, and shaped by God's love and grace. By sharing the story of how **our** FAMILY has grown to be, our hope is not for the FAMILY SHRUB to chop down the FAMILY TREE. Instead, through the **"shrub not a tree"** philosophy, our hope is to help **other** FAMILIES embrace the *growth* and *intentional blessing* of **their** FAMILY, while helping them to also achieve God's **purpose** for planting **their** family.

Whether our FAMILIES grow to be more of a SHRUB or more of a TREE, we are ALL a part of God's kingdom and His one big FAMILY!

Two Moms, One Name

Not being able to give birth to our children, we wanted to find another way to give them a part of us besides the love, qualities, and life lessons we share with them. The solution: Micah's middle name is Andrew, my husband's first name, and the girls' middle name is Rae, which is my middle name.

While navigating the process of adopting our three daughters, we gathered information from their birth certificates. While reviewing the documents, I noticed the middle name of their birth mother, to which I immediately started to cry. Only through God's design do the two of us share the same middle name, Rae - two moms, one name. Our daughters now have the same middle name as both of their mothers - their birth mother and their adoptive mother. While crying at this discovery, He revealed to me the purpose for our families and the meaningful ways in which our relationships fulfill that purpose as they overlap and intertwine. In that moment, I was a witness to God's faithful plan and the power of His mighty hand. When we remember to surrender our lives willingly and completely to Him in all circumstances, we can ALL be witnesses to that plan.

As their biological and adoptive mothers, Sami and I both love our children and want the best possible life for them. On many occasions, Sami has thanked us for giving them the life that she isn't able to provide. In all reality, we wouldn't be able to give them that life if it wasn't for her. We're beyond grateful for our journey as it was through that journey and our devotion to the Lord that God gifted us with life's greatest blessing…OUR family! Sami is now a part of our family and we will continue to foster a relationship between her and the daughters we share as long as it remains appropriate and healthy for everyone.

Special Messages from Our Family Shrub

"When I was asked to share the journey of foster care and adoption from my own perspective, my mind went blank. I had no idea where to start, what parts to include, or where to end, but here is what I came up with. My name is Sami. I'm a mom of six amazing children that went into foster care in early 2019. I still remember that day like it was yesterday. I have three boys who live with their biological grandmother who doesn't let me see nor talk to them, and I have three girls who live with their adoptive family who let me see pictures and videos of all their amazing adventures they get to go on. They also make it possible for me to see the girls in person on occasion. When the kids were placed in foster care, I was a single mom who didn't really have much help. When I did ask for help, I got told, "everything will work out for the best." Ironically, I guess they were right in some ways. I eventually decided it would be best for the girls to be adopted because I knew I could never give them the life they deserved. Although I know I made the right decision, there isn't a day that goes by that I don't think about them and their brothers who still live with their biological grandmother. I often wonder about all the "firsts" I am missing and continue to miss out on, but having children in foster care and then going through the process of adoption has really changed my life and my outlook on it. My three girls have two moms that love them. They have two families that care for them and only want what's best for them. This adoption situation could be so different because there are many families everyday whose children are adopted and never get to see them again. I am forever grateful for the family that chose to love and care for my three amazing girls. I'm grateful to them for having the hearts they do to include me in the girls' life. Although I'm so happy for them, there are times when I feel very alone. I went from spending everyday with my kids and having this life that was all about them to not even having a routine anymore. I feel guilty about going out and having fun because they aren't here with me. I still, to this day, have some guilt when planning or even just going and doing something that they would have loved and enjoyed doing. Life is slowly getting easier as time goes by, but that is because I keep telling myself that I will get my time with them again to go on adventures, make memories, and maybe make up for lost time. I'm hoping that by sharing my own perspective as a biological mother who wants only the best life for her children, I'm able to provide some insight to those who may have misunderstandings or their own opinions about families who have children in foster care or who make the very difficult decision for their children to be adopted. Every family and every situation is different. The best way to support any family's journey is to better understand their story. Hopefully you now have a better understanding of ours." To Lyric, Ryder, Andrew, Kinzie, Serenity, and Luna; I love you and miss you, and there is never a day that goes by that I don't think about all of you."
~ Mommy Sami - Kinzie, Luna, and Serenity's Biological Mom

"Adoption can be both a blessing and a heartache at the same time. I am a Grandma of eight amazing grandchildren. I love all my grands more than they know. Shortly after Micah was born, we knew his birth parents were not able to take care of him, so he was placed into foster care. He was with two different families who were both wonderful. Although we were grateful that he was in great care, I felt guilty and so sad that he wasn't able to be with us, but with my age, I knew I wasn't able to care for him. Because neither of his parents were able to care for him, Micah's plan changed from reunification to adoption. When I found out that he was going to be adopted by my nephew and his wife, it was the blessing I had prayed for, as it would keep him close to the family. Knowing he would be raised in a loving family that wanted to start a family of their own made it even more special." **~ Grandma Kathy - Micah's Biological Grandma**

Special Messages from Our Family Shrub

"Two words that come to mind when I think of the love I have for all of my grandchildren are affinity and boundless. Although I'm not connected to some of my grandchildren by blood, I am connected to them by love, and it's a love that I give and receive without end. This journey of adoption has been an opportunity for me to experience a feeling of love far beyond anything I ever thought possible. All of our grandchildren bring so much joy to our lives. Thank you, Ashley and Andrew, for your unselfish love that has allowed me, and our family, this experience. Remember to trust that in all ways God's plan is greater than ours. This grandma is forever grateful for the family we've grown to be and will love all my grandchildren for an eternity. I have been blessed."
~ Grandma Gail - Adoptive Grandma

"When I heard my daughter and her husband were going to possibly adopt, I was a little uncertain how to feel about it. I had one biological grandson at the time, and I knew how I felt in my heart about him. I had thought frequently how I would feel about a grandson who was not biological. Well, it was like love at first sight, and it didn't take long to feel the same kind of love for Micah as I felt for my first grandson. I was very fortunate to be able to help out when Ashley and Andrew needed it. The more time I spent with Micah, the more I realized that this little boy had so much love to give and was so deserving of that love in return. When Ashley and Andrew decided to adopt three little girls, I knew in my heart that they would receive the same love from me just as my two grandsons received. The one thing I have truly learned through this journey is this; whether a child is biological or not, they have a lot of love to give, and they need to receive that same love back. They're deserving of that love. Afterall, it's not the children's fault for the circumstances in their lives. When they all moved to Florida, I think it was harder for me than them. When they moved, it was as if a piece of myself was missing. Because of the way our family has grown to be, I now have two grandsons and three granddaughters, and I love each and every one of them the same - they are all my grandkids. God has given me a gift; a gift to see the face of Jesus in each and every one of them." **~ Grandpa Randy - Adoptive Grandpa**

"God's blessing…the gift of a child. There is no difference if a grandchild is biological or adopted. The love you have for them is the same. Even before Andrew and Ashley adopted the children and were caring for them through foster care, we cared for them no differently than we would any other child; love has no boundaries. For these children, we are forever grateful and will always love them deeply." ~ Papa David and Grandma Kim - Adoptive Grandparents." **~ Papa David and Grandma Kim - Adoptive Grandparents**

"Being a foster parent isn't about being the "best" parent ever, and it isn't about helping "bus-loads" of kids. It's about being present for just the child(ren) in your care at that time when they need you the most. It's about being the safe place for them where they can eat, sleep, and play. It's about learning from them just as much as they are learning from you. If you're new to foster care, you WILL make mistakes, just like every other "first-time" parent, and that's okay! Even families who have a lot of experience fostering still make mistakes, but at the end of the day we're just trying to do what's best for the children when they're in our care. Nobody's foster journey is the same. Your journey may include one child, ten children, or 100 children. Don't let the fear of "what-ifs" and the feeling of "I can't provide care for as many kids as the other foster families can" prevent you from being a part of any one child's story. Start the conversation, talk with real foster families, learn the realities and the truths, and don't let all the misconceptions shut down the idea of fostering before it even has a chance to start." **~ Michaela & Brad - Foster Parents**

Our Ask to You

Our ask to you is to please consider growing your own Family Shrub by opening your minds to the different ways in which your own family can grow, and to open your hearts and homes to children in foster care and/or to those in need of a stable and nurturing family unit through adoption. To start, you may consider 1) reaching out to your local county social|human services to gather basic information to help you discern if becoming a full-time foster family and/or an adoptive family is an appropriate fit for you. There is no obligation or commitment by simply gathering information and asking questions. If becoming a full-time foster family and/or an adoptive family is not a good fit for you at this time, or ever, you may then consider 2) becoming a part-time respite care provider who supports the foster community by providing short-term care for foster children. If becoming a part-time respite care provider is not a good fit for you at this time, or ever, you may then consider 3) asking for simple ways in which you can support the foster community and/or at-risk families in your area. From donating items to running an errand, there are endless ways to support families in your local community. If that's not an option for you, you can 4) pray; pray for all the children and families around the world like ours who have been impacted by infertility, foster care, and/or adoption. Last, but not least, we ask that you 5) help us celebrate all families by snapping a photo of your family, with or without our book, and sharing it on social media using #aSHRUBnotaTREE and/or #GodsOneBigFamily. Don't forget to tag us on Instagram and Facebook @aSHRUBnotaTREE. Whether our FAMILIES grow to be more of a SHRUB or more of a TREE, we are ALL a part of God's kingdom and His one big FAMILY!

There are numerous local, national, and global organizations that focus their efforts on supporting those impacted by infertility, adoption, and/or foster care. We encourage you to consider connecting with and/or collaborating with organizations that can support and serve the needs of your unique journey. Below are just a few of the many organizations that we have collaborated with during our journey and continue to promote and support today.

Infertility
Resolve – The National Infertility Association
www.Resolve.org

Everlasting Hope
www.RaisingEverlastingHope.org

Adoption
Adults Adopting Special Kids; a program offered through Catholic Charities North Dakota
www.AASKnd.org

Congressional Coalition on Adoption Institute
www.CCAInstitute.org

Foster Care
Be a Foster Podcast
www.Anchor.fm/beafoster

Nexus-PATH Family Healing
www.nexusfamilyhealing.org

FosterMore
www.FosterMore.org

Meet the Author ~ Ashley Rae

As a *faithful servant leader,* **Ashley Rae** (Klinger) lives a life devoted to serving God's people, rather than being served by them. As a passionate **matriarch** to her family, she's a supportive wife to her husband, Andrew, a grateful and loving mom to their four adopted children, and a humble **advocate** for children and families around the world.

A **philanthropist** at heart, Ashley Rae is an active community member, giving back where God calls her to serve. As a 2008 *cancer survivor,* she founded the Cope Well Foundation to serve the needs of the cancer community, which she represented as Mrs. North Dakota International 2016. In 2019, amid their journey with *infertility, adoption,* and *foster care,* Ashley Rae cofounded - with Andrew, the BE A FOSTER Movement to serve the needs of the foster community. She proudly represented this initiative as Mrs. International 2020. In addition to their involvement with the *in/fertility, adoption,* and *foster care* communities, Ashley Rae and her family enjoy promoting a variety of community organizations, especially those that support military veterans.

Born with the spirit of an **entrepreneur**, Ashley Rae is the founder and owner of It's Her Brand Enterprises, a lifestyle empowerment and development business where she strives to help young ladies and women live purposeful, intentional, engaged, and faith-filled lives. She has 21 years of marketing, branding, media, and writing experience, 18 years of business development experience, 12 years of nonprofit development and professional speaking experience, 10 years of personal and professional coaching experience, 5 years of platform development and pageant coaching experience as the founder of Be International Pageant Coaching; and 5 years of publishing and editing experience as the founder of It's Her Brand Magazine and I'm International Magazine. Her vast array of experience has equipped her with the ability to understand how to develop meaningful messages and life-changing platforms, while appropriately and effectively sharing and promoting those messages and platforms with audiences around the world.

Among many other personal and professional achievements and recognitions, Ashley Rae was most recently selected as the **American Mothers, Inc. 2021 North Dakota Mother of the Year** (www.AmericanMothers.org) and as a **Congressional Coalition on Adoption Institute's 2020 Angels in Adoption Honoree** (www.CCAInstitute.org).

Originally from North Dakota, Ashley Rae and her family moved to Daytona Beach, Florida in 2022 where they currently reside with their two puppies, Bella and Barklee.

What did they think about it?

"As a fellow foster and adoptive mom, I know you will resonate with the way the author describes trusting God fully to build their family through their complete surrender and trust in Him. His plans are always better than ours, and if you are hesitant about taking the step toward building your family through adoption, this book is a must-read." ~ Leanna Ihry | Foster and Adoptive Mom

"Transparency, letting go of the ego, focusing on what is in the best interest of the child/ren; this book has all that and more. It is a concise, easy to read, road map focusing on something much larger than any one of us. Nurturing children, while fostering relationships with biological families, strengthens child/rens sense of belonging, while building bridges to plant those roots deep, resulting in strong, healthy children who know exactly who they are and where they come from." ~ Mary Langley | Retired Social Worker, Adopted

"A Shrub Not a Tree offers a compassionate and inspirational message on adoption, as experienced by the author, Ashley Rae Klinger. Ashley openly discusses her, and her husband's emotional journey that led them to foster parenting and eventually adoption. Drawing strength and guidance from her spiritual faith, she is able to personally experience that family is defined by love, which, in adoption, includes multiple family members. The book offers sections specifically for youth and parents, which is a tremendous support for the whole adoption family. This book is a wonderful addition for all involved in adoption." ~ Charley Joyce | MSW, Adoptive Grandparent, Co-author of "Behavior with a Purpose" and Retired Clinical Social Worker

Ashley and Andrew are truly an inspiring couple. Their faith in God is unwavering and bleeds over into the lives of those around them. Ashley and I have shared our heartbreaks in dealing with infertility. Sadly, it is something so many women go through and end up feeling like they are "less than" in some way. Nothing could be further from the truth. I have watched her grieve the "what could have been" and turned the circumstances into not only a positive, but a mission in life. My family is blended, which comes with its own set of challenges. Sometimes it is difficult to explain to children why certain things happen. This book will help so many to normalize all different types of families and to embrace the differences and circumstances God places on our path." ~ Lindsay Porten | Blended Family, RN, LPC

Meet the Illustrators ~ Quynh & Christopher

QBN Studios is a small illustration studio located in Vernon, Connecticut. Owners, Quynh Nguyen and Christopher MacCoy, are passionate about helping authors fulfill their dreams and bring their words to life. QBN Studio's goal aims to create an immersive experience for their audiences to tumble headfirst into imaginary worlds. Follow Quynh and Christopher on Instagram @qbnstudios for the latest updates on illustrations, books, and other projects.

"From the initial creative session to the final preparations, Quynh and Christopher made this process easy and enjoyable. We searched for months for the right illustrator to help us bring our message to life. We were relieved when we connected with this dynamic duo. We would recommend them to anyone in need of a high-quality, professional illustrator who is creative, reliable, and friendly." ~ Ashley Rae Klinger.

"During our journey through *infertility*, *adoption*, and *foster care*, God sowed in our hearts the **Family Shrub** and the **"shrub not a tree"** philosophy to help **our** family and others see the *growth* and *intentional blessing* of **our** family. **Our** family may be more of a SHRUB than a TREE, but this is the family **we** have grown to be; a family groomed, pruned, and shaped by God's love and grace. By sharing the story of how **our** family has grown to be through the **"shrub not a tree"** philosophy, our hope is to help **other** families see the *growth* and *intentional blessing* of **their** family while helping them to also achieve God's **purpose** for planting **their** family, so they can **grow together** and **reach their maturity and full blooming potential**; whether that be as a **Family Shrub** or as a **Family Tree**." ~ Ashley Rae (Klinger)

"Eye-opening! **A Shrub Not a Tree** is astounding! As a blended family of six, we struggled ourselves with how to define our newly blended family, but in **A Shrub Not a Tree** Ashley breaks down this life-altering concept and brings freedom and hope to all families, no matter how they've grown to be! This book is a must-have for all family libraries!" ~ Brad and Elisha Daugherty | Blended Family of 6

"I have 24 years of experience as a Foster Care Case Manager, working with children in foster care, their families, foster parents, and adoptive parents. I found this book to be an amazing resource for any child and adult alike, whether adoptive or biological. The depiction of **A Shrub Not a Tree** is a heartfelt message that speaks to the uniqueness of these families but at the same time the similarities as well. It shows how working together as a team can have a positive outcome for children, helping them achieve their greatest potential. How acceptance of biological family members can aide in the healthy development of the children and provide the biological parents with a sense of worthiness. Foster/adoptive children can see themselves in the pages of this book and have a better understanding of their journey. It is an inspiring story of love, faith, trust, purpose, and acceptance that can lead to meaningful family conversations. I highly recommend it." ~ Jacki Lund | Social Worker

"I absolutely love the concept of **A Shrub Not a Tree.** It is an inspiring, true story that I can read with our daughter, but it also has a component for my husband and I to read, learn, and discuss together. The way in which the author describes how her family and other families are more like a shrub than a tree resonated with me, as we too added to our family through adoption. The message in this book had me nodding in agreement many times as the author talked about her faith and who each of us are to God. Yes, we are ALL a part of God's family! Our chosen daughter is an intentional blessing from God, just as her children are. Foster care and adoption can be very difficult, and I needed the reminder that we need to pick the weeds of negativity, as the weeds can strangle the joy that God wants me to experience. Ashley, thank you for sharing your journey, for being God's light, and for helping me to grow in my faith through your family's experiences and your words. I pray that as many others read this book, they too will understand and accept God's love for them." ~ Robyn and Nancy Yon | Foster and Adoptive Parents

"Whether our families grow to be more of a shrub or more of a tree, we are all a part of God's kingdom and His one big family!"

www.aSHRUBnotaTREE.com

www.ingramcontent.com/pod-product-compliance
Lightning Source LLC
Chambersburg PA
CBHW040723060526

44119CB00083B/304